The Pinta Trail
in the Texas Hill Country

*Traditional research aided by new technologies
reveals the forgotten path of a historic Texas trail.*

By Jefferson Morgenthaler

Mockingbird Books
201 Second Street
Boerne, TX 78006
www.mockingbirdbooks.com
contact@mockingbirdbooks.com

Introduction

Beginning in 1845, German immigrants of the Adelsverein colonization company became the first settlers to venture significantly north of San Antonio. From their first staging ground at New Braunfels, they made plans for a second at Fredericksburg, a way station on the journey to their promised lands north of the Llano River.

The best-known pathway into the frontier to the north was the Pinta Trail, said to be an ancient native trace. The trail began at San Antonio, crossed the Guadalupe River near today's Sisterdale, and ventured north at least as far as the vicinity of Fredericksburg. It had been used by itinerant natives, Spanish soldiers, and Texas Rangers for transit to and from the Texas Hill Country. Once adopted by the German immigrants, it remained the principal gateway to the northern German settlements—and to the frontier beyond—until the early 1850s, when pioneers built a new and less arduous route known as the Fredericksburg Road.

Around 1854, traffic on the lower Pinta Trail ceased when a cutoff from the Fredericksburg Road opened a convenient connection from Boerne to the upper Pinta Trail near Sisterdale. The Pinta Trail continued to be used above that settlement for a period of time, but a new road from Sisterdale through Luckenbach to Fredericksburg emerged and that development, along with increasing reliance on the Fredericksburg Road, doomed the upper Pinta Trail by the 1880s.

The location and destination of the Pinta Trail has not been previously understood. Significant misinformation has accumulated over the years. New historical research has brought greater clarity to the topic than was possible before. This pamphlet updates and corrects existing scholarship on the trail, adding a solid foundation of fact to accounts that have long depended on legend.

The Pinta Trail

Fredericksburg

U.S. 290

Old No. 9

FM 1376

FM 473

Comfort

Sisterdale

Guadalupe River

Pinta Trail

Boerne

Hwy 46

Interstate 10

Camp Bullis

Loop 1604

San Antonio

Researching the Pinta Trail

The only reference to the Pinta Trail in documents from the Spanish and Mexican governance of Texas during the 18th and 19th centuries is in an 1829 map done by (or, more likely, for) Stephen F. Austin to present to the president of Mexico, showing a "Puerta Pinta" northwest of San Antonio between Salado Creek and Cibolo Creek. After Texas achieved independence from Mexico, and after the Adelsverein's German colonists settled in the Hill Country, an 1850 map of German settlements done by Hermann Willke clearly marks the "Camino Pintas" coming out of San Antonio. An 1857 Gillespie County survey map shows a dotted line crossing the Pedernales River and running east of Fredericksburg, labeled "Pinto Trail"; that trail mark was traced and re-traced on Gillespie County survey maps as late as 1918, long after the trail had vanished.[1]

There are other mentions on large-scale official maps, but not many. Combined, these maps reveal some basics about the trail: north of San Antonio, it generally followed Salado Creek; it crossed Cibolo Creek about five miles east of Boerne; it crossed the Guadalupe River about where FM 1376 does today, near Sisterdale, though it did not approach the Guadalupe along that road. The trail passed through today's Sisterdale, extending to a point near, but east of, Fredericksburg. Among other revelations, the large-scale maps put the kibosh on traditional theories that the Main Streets of Boerne and Fredericksburg are off-kilter from north-south because they were laid on top of the trail. It appears that they were built on an angle for other reasons, such as the course of an adjacent creek.

Turning from large-scale official maps to smaller, informal items found in the files and online collections of the Texas General Land Office, there is a tattered October 1841 sketch inked by the legendary John C. "Jack" Hays of surveys done northwest of San Antonio. It shows about 35 surveys along Balcones Creek, Cibolo Creek, and an unnamed drainage that is Salado Creek. A dotted line parallels Salado Creek and crosses Balcones Creek near its confluence with the Cibolo, and is labeled "Pinta Trail." A sketch done by surveyor John James circa 1842 shows the "Pintas road leading from San Antonio NW," marking it as it crosses the Cibolo below Balcones Creek. A scrap of a survey sketch done by John James in September 1846 shows a dotted line crossing Cibolo Creek at Post Oak Creek and following that stream upward; that same line appears just to the north and continues beyond the future Sisterdale on an October 1847 sketch done by surveyor Charles deMontel. We know from other sources that the line is the Pinta Trail.[2]

In addition to its collection of maps and sketches, the TGLO maintains physical files, and a separate online database, of small-scale original land survey files. Many of the early surveys—especially those performed between San Antonio and Fredericksburg by Jack Hays, John James, William Friedrich, Charles de Montel, and Joseph Tivy from 1839 through 1847—noted trail locations on sketches and in field notes. Those locations can be translated to the larger-scale historic survey maps, platting trail points across counties.

Digital Geographical Information Systems developed over the last decade allow the trail to be mapped with much greater accuracy. Measurements taken by early surveyors can be replicated closely onto satellite images and digital maps. Unfortunately, the inherent inaccuracy of early surveys renders any

John C. "Jack" Hays

attempt at precision meaningless. The original surveys were accurate only to the nearest vara—33.33 inches—and even that generous standard was sometimes not met. Many surveys along the Pinta Trail were executed long before the lands were safe for settlement; armed surveyors may have been distracted by the need to watch out for Comanches. Original survey monuments were less-than-permanent trees, creeks, mounds of rocks, and the occasional trail. Sometimes surveyors gave precise measurements for where trails crossed survey bounda-

ries, sometimes they gave round numbers that look like esti-
mates, and sometimes they merely put a dotted line on the
survey sketch.

There are issues beyond the inherent inaccuracy of early
surveys. Trails shift. When a rainstorm turns a trail into a mud
hole, travelers move their tracks to one side or another. When
a pioneer builds a cabin, the trail may detour to pass by his
homestead. When someone locates an easier creek crossing,
the trail moves to that point. For example, we know that Pinta
Trail travelers frequently used the Guadalupe River ford near
Sister Creek but sometimes used another ford almost three
miles to the east, at Cypress Bend.[3]

Still, the degree of accuracy that we can achieve today is
important. Knowing approximately where the Pinta Trail was
on the date that it was surveyed is a major improvement, and
is a luxury that we do not have with most historic Texas trails.
Platting the trail with greater precision allows us to brush
away errors and myths that attend it, and offers the potential
for archaeological discoveries.

Past Interpretations

Even though Willke's 1850 map clearly showed the Pinta
Trail, copies of the map are not in wide circulation, and the
location of the trail in relation to today's landmarks is not im-
mediately obvious upon viewing the map. The other existing
large-scale maps and sketches of the trail are more obscure
and more difficult to interpret. As a result, few if any historians
have accurately determined the correct location of the Pinta
Trail. Nonetheless, we have not shirked from behaving as if we
did—and that "we" includes the author. One generation of con-
ventional Pinta Trail wisdom had it running west of Boerne to

Comfort, then somehow extending to Fredericksburg—probably along today's U.S. Highway 87. That's not the case. It is a welcoming route, but there is no evidence of an old trail in that direction.[4]

Another popular version of the Pinta Trail has it following FM 1376 from Boerne through Sisterdale and onward to Fredericksburg. That theory is wrong. The Pinta Trail was five miles east of Boerne. The road that became FM 1376 was built after Boerne's founding in 1852 and appears to have been the death knell for the lower Pinta Trail.[5]

It is still said that the Pinta Trail extended as far as the old Spanish presidio on the San Saba River—an antiquity that, along with the lost silver mines at Los Almagres, has generated its share of legends. While it's certain that Spaniards used one or more trails to make the trip between San Antonio and the presidio and mission, there is no historical record evidencing that the Pinta Trail was involved, at least not above the Guadalupe River. In fact, once the Pinta crossed the Pedernales River, it is uncertain where it went, though two possibilities—one vague, one more certain—are mentioned below.[6]

Among the resources perpetuating the romantic but unsupported Presidio San Saba claim are two markers placed by the Texas Historical Commission commemorating the Pinta Trail. One is in Gillespie County, on U.S. Highway 290, about five miles east of downtown Fredericksburg. The marker was probably placed on an old wagon trace, but two 1840 Jack Hays surveys mark the trail a half-mile to the west. The other marker is in Kendall County, on Ammann Road, about five miles east of downtown Boerne. This marker is near visible remnants of an old trail; an 1846 survey by Joseph Tivy puts the Pinta Trail a mere two hundred yards west. Both markers claim that the trail reached the presidio, and their apparent authority has led people to accept that dubious claim.[7]

The Pinta Trail in the 18th Century

The name "Pinta Trail," or one of its variants—Pientas, Paint, Pindas, Pinto—does not appear in old Spanish or Mexican maps and documents. But the trail—if not its name—shows up as early as 1767, when the Marqués de Rubí conducted an inspection of Spanish frontier presidios. The outpost farthest north was the Presidio San Saba. Rubí visited the admittedly miserable post for ten days in July, approaching it from the southwest. When he departed, he set his sights on San Antonio, five days away. Setting forth, he crossed Los Chanes River (the Llano), Los Pedernales Arroyo (the Pedernales River), then picked up El Mitote Arroyo (Cypress Creek) and followed it downstream to the Alarcón River (the Guadalupe), where the town of Comfort is today. From there, Rubí proceeded east along the Guadalupe; his engineer and map maker, Nicolas Lafora, referred to the river, "whose course to the east follows the road somewhat apart from it for five leagues." The reference to a road is intriguing, suggesting that they were following a visible trail.[8]

According to Lafora, Rubí traveled four leagues (10.4 miles, using a 2.6 mile league) in the hills above the river before fording it at the "Primer Paso." His calculation of distance puts him almost exactly at the Pinta Trail ford on the Guadalupe (near West Sister Creek and today's Sisterdale), and his subsequent calculations tie surprisingly well to other Pinta Trail landmarks, especially considering that Lafora estimated the distances in round leagues with only occasional half-leagues: 5.2 miles to El Rosario Arroyo (Wasp Creek, actually about 4 miles, depending on the route taken); 2.6 more miles to Las Mojarritas Arroyo (Sabinas Creek, actually about 2.2 miles), another 2.6 miles to Atascocito Arroyo (Spring Creek, at the correct distance); then a small pass (where Post Oak Creek cuts through the ridge known as the "Balcones" above Cibolo Creek); another 5.2 miles to Balcones Arroyo (Balcones

First Page of Rubí's Diary

Creek or Cibolo Creek near their confluence; the best-documented crossing was on Cibolo Creek at about 5 miles); Los Alamitos Arroyo in 6.5 miles (Salado Creek at that distance); that much distance again to another small pass (where today's

Northwest Military Drive cuts through the Balcones Escarpment north of Texas State Highway Loop 1604); and finally 18.2 miles to San Antonio de Bexar (from the pass at the escarpment to the steps of San Fernando Cathedral is about 16 direct miles).[9]

We know, thanks to the Texas land surveys, Willke's map, and other resources, that Rubí's route below the Guadalupe, as described by Lafora, is the Pinta Trail. Six creeks—Wasp, Sabinas, Spring, Post Oak, Cibolo (just below the Balcones), and Salado—are indelible marks of the Pinta Trail between the Guadalupe and San Antonio. Only one other notable landmark was omitted: Comanche Spring near Salado Creek.[10]

Rubí's travels make it clear that the Pinta Trail was in existence, if not named, as early as 1767. It seems likely that it was a native pathway of greater age. Perhaps it pre-dated the appearance of Apaches in central Texas around the 17th century, or the arrival of their deadly enemies, the Comanches, in the 18th century. Perhaps it was used earlier by itinerant Jumanos on their trading expeditions through central Texas. At this point, without archaeological support, it is impossible to say.

The Pinta Trail in the 19th Century

When the Republic of Texas began issuing land grant certificates, or scrip, in 1838, a land boom began in San Antonio, the gateway to the frontier. Jack Hays was already a Texas Ranger and quickly adopted the dual identity of a surveyor, putting his team to work alternately fighting Comanches and staking out lands. The year 1839 found him on the Pedernales River in the vicinity of the future Fredericksburg, where, under the command of Col. Henry W. Karnes, he routed a band of Comanches led by Chief Isomania. It is more than likely that Hays used the Pinta Trail to explore, survey, and fight. As he became familiar with the trail, and with favorable places for settlements along its route, it was only natural that Hays's surveying crew would mark off familiar lands along the Guadalupe River, the Pedernales River, and beyond to the Llano and San Saba. These lands along abundant watercourses were premium locations for future settlement.[11]

The Pinta Trail makes its first cartographical appearance on Kendall County survey number 1, performed in 1839 by Jack Hays, which shows the "Paint Road" crossing the Guadalupe River below Sisterdale, at Rubí's Primer Paso. It is widely repeated that Hays and his band of Texas Rangers fought Comanche Chief Yellow Wolf near that location in the June 1844 battle of Walker's Creek, but Hays's own account does not mention the trail, even though he had been marking it on surveys for five years. After Hays's 1839 initial survey and until 1847, 35 more individual land surveys identify the Pinta Trail.[12]

The trail appears first outside the context of survey maps as the "Camino Pintas" on Willke's 1850 map of German settlements in Texas. While Willke's map is not an official survey map, Willke was a surveyor by profession; his map displays survey boundaries accurately along the trails and appears to be based on official land surveys done by Hays and others.[13]

By 1845 the Adelsverein colonization company had begun building a town northeast of San Antonio at New Braunfels, a stopping point on the way to a land grant far north beyond the Llano River. It had been almost a century since anyone had tried to gain a foothold more than a few miles beyond San Antonio—the Spanish had built their mission and presidio on the San Saba in 1757, but that audacious experiment had collapsed in a dozen years under intense Comanche pressure.[14]

Adelsverein leader John Meusebach set forth from New Braunfels in August 1845 to find a location for a second settlement—the village that would be named Fredericksburg—

John Meusebach

about two-thirds of the way to the Germans' land grant. Meusebach and Jack Hays had met that summer, when the Adelsverein awarded Hays a special rifle in recognition of his efforts on behalf of the colonists. It is likely that Hays—the recognized local authority on geography north of San Antonio—influenced his choice of townsites. Hays was optimistic about the prospects for peaceful relations between the Germans and the Comanches and he had counseled Meusebach's predecessor, Prince Carl of Solms-Braunfels, about the impossibility of reaching the colony lands beyond the Llano without establishing way stations where the colonists could rest and recruit on the journey.[15]

As the crow flies, Fredericksburg was 60 miles from New Braunfels, and 65 from San Antonio, but the route that the settlers took from New Braunfels to Fredericksburg worked out to be about 75 miles of rough trail, much of it over rocky ridges and deep ravines. Meusebach made the trip in August 1845 on horseback, then in January 1846 he sent out a team of men to widen and improve the trail in anticipation of immigrants' wagons that would depart New Braunfels in April. From New Braunfels, the route followed the east-west Nacogdoches Road (a Spanish Camino Real) to a point about 15 miles northeast of old San Antonio; as the road began to dip south toward the town, Meusebach instead continued west, crossing Cibolo Creek (which runs north-south at that point), turning up Salado Creek just south of the Balcones Escarpment and following it upstream past Medicine Wall to intercept the Pinta Trail as it approached from the southwest. The trail then proceeded north along Salado Creek to Comanche Spring, crossed Cibolo Creek again (on an east-west stretch of the creek), angling northwest to cross the Guadalupe River near the future Sisterdale. Above Sisterdale the trail again angled northwest, away from today's roads, meeting the Pedernales River near the future site of the Mormon colony of Zodiac, about two miles east of the U.S. Army's future Fort Martin Scott on Baron's Creek, and about 4.5 miles east of central Fredericksburg.[16]

In 1840 Jack Hays marked the Pinta Trail crossing the Pedernales near the top of the first inverted U loop east of Baron's Creek, and he confirmed that point in the sketch of an adjacent survey in 1846. The remnants of an old bridge remain in the vicinity. From there, the trail continues north, to the east of Fredericksburg. Another 1846 Jack Hays survey places the ford about a half-mile farther upstream, but that is not a survey of a tract actually crossed by the trail. On Willke's 1850 map, the road to Fredericksburg, derived from the Pinta Trail, crosses the river upstream at Baron's Creek and follows it to Fredericksburg; apparently the preferred ford shifted west to be nearer the settlement.[17]

When Meusebach first reached the Pedernales in August 1845, the choice lands along the river had already been surveyed and patented; many of the surveys had been done by Jack Hays five years earlier. For his new settlement of Fredericksburg, Meusebach chose lands along two creeks above the Pedernales—soon dubbed Baron's Creek and Town Creek.[18]

The Pinta Trail remained the only route to Fredericksburg for about a decade. In January 1847 German traveler Ferdinand Roemer traveled from New Braunfels to Fredericksburg. Riding the Nacogdoches Road west from New Braunfels, he took the cutoff to the Pinta Trail, finding the cutoff more visible than the onward road to San Antonio because a number of loaded wagons had recently gone to Fredericksburg. Roemer called his route from that point the "Pinto Trail, selected with Indian sagacity, which is the only convenient passage from the undulating prairies of western Texas to the interior of the rocky tableland, cut up by deep ravines and fissured river valleys." Roemer's only apparent deviation from the standard Pinta Trail route was at the Guadalupe River, which he forded at Cypress Bend, three miles east of the usual location. It took Roemer four days to make the journey and, although his journal makes it clear that the trip was not without its challenges, he described the Pinta Trail as "in general as good as any similar road in Texas of equal distance, now that improvements instituted by the Verein have been carried out."[19]

In June 1849, U.S. Army Lieutenant Francis T. Bryan followed the trail to Fredericksburg. Though he does not name the Pinta, his expedition to explore a road from San Antonio to El Paso tracked key milestones: Cibolo Creek, Post Oak Spring, Spring Creek, Sabinas Creek ("the Sabinal"), Wasp Creek, the Guadalupe River, Sister Creeks, Grape Creek, the Pedernales. He reported a shortcut to the right of the trail beyond Sisterdale, but calls it "entirely impracticable for any wagon or wheeled vehicle." This may have been something akin to the route that FM 1376 takes today above Sisterdale.[20]

When U.S. Boundary Commissioner John R. Bartlett traveled from San Antonio to El Paso in October 1850, he decided to take the northern route through Fredericksburg instead of the southern route, which "had been more traveled and was better known." Leaving San Antonio, he passed Comanche Spring; the next day he reached Sabinas Creek ("Sabine Creek"), crossing it the next morning. His next stop was at the Guadalupe River crossing, where he encountered the home and person of Ottmar von Behr, whom he called "Mr. Berne" and who kept an aromatic pet javelina. His route beyond Sisterdale is vague, except for crossing high ridges and beautiful valleys, eventually fording the Pedernales River ("the river Piedernales") near Zodiac, which had been established in 1847 close to the Pinta Trail ford. He then checked in at Fort Martin

Scott, one mile west on Baron's Creek (one mile was his estimate; the distance was actually closer to two direct miles);
Bartlett identified the fort as "the most extreme post on the
frontier." Two miles beyond was Fredericksburg (again, his estimate; actually about 2.6 direct miles to the town center),
where he found that "the stores were filled with goods adapted
to the Indian trade, as the place is on the very borders of civi-
lization and resorted to by numbers of the Indian tribes con-
tiguous."[21]

The lower trail as far as the Guadalupe soon fell out of
favor. When Frederick Law Olmsted traveled from San Antonio
to Sisterdale in 1854, he first "traveled loosely over the prairies, only keeping [the horses'] heads toward the north." Soon
he reached "the Cibolo, at the road-crossing, where a town
named Börne had been laid out, and a few houses built." This
puts Olmstead on or near another trail originally known as the
San Saba Road, which passed a half-mile west of Boerne, or a
variant of that road, soon known as the Fredericksburg Road,
which passed directly through Boerne; the Pinta Trail was five
miles to the east. The next day he crossed a rugged ridge to
the valley of the Guadalupe; his description is scanty, but the
likelihood is that by 1854, two years after Boerne was founded,
a direct road from Boerne to Sisterdale—now FM 1376—had
been cleared, creating an easier and shorter route to the Guadalupe. The establishment of Boerne—where a traveler might
find a warm dinner and a dry bed—likely prompted the shift
of the preferred route away from the Pinta Trail, but it is impossible to know.[22]

Olmsted took a second trip from San Antonio to Sisterdale shortly after his first. This time he took a different path:
"the old, now disused, Fredericksburg road, which passes by
Comanche spring." That would, of course, be the Pinta Trail.

Olmsted reported that "the old road-marks were grown over with grass, and quite indistinct." Olmstead struck to the east toward Cibolo Creek, seeking a trail that was supposed to reach the Guadalupe River about ten miles below Sisterdale. As it turned out, Olmsted and his party got lost and, after a difficult time crossing the Guadalupe, ended up at the Currie's Creek settlement. From there they made it westward to Sisterdale, where his companion accidentally set a large amount of the landscape on fire. After a week in camp at Sisterdale, he "rode over the rocky hills again, and followed the Comanche Spring road to San Antonio."[23]

It's not obvious why Olmsted would not return by the less arduous route that he used on his first trip to Sisterdale, but the adventurer and explorer in him probably demanded that he do a better job of cross-country travel on his return than he had on his approach. For present purposes the relevant point is that above Comanche Spring Olmsted did not use the Pinta Trail on any of the four legs to and from Sisterdale. The lower trail was "old, now disused."[24]

That was not the case with the upper Pinta Trail above the Guadalupe. Today's FM 1376 generally and briefly follows the original route from the river through Sisterdale, onward to where FM 473 turns west, and for about three-tenths of a mile above that intersection. At that point, the creek and the old trail bore northwest up the West Sister Creek Valley, but today's road shifts slightly east and begins to ascend rocky hills on its way to Luckenbach.[25]

We know that the upper trail was at least partly in use as late as 1879, when C. G. Vogel, secretary of the Texas Immigration and Land Company, filed paperwork with the Texas General Land Office showing his company's intent to establish the official town of Sisterdale near the mouth of West Sister Creek Valley, along the "Paint Road." Those plans never came to fruition; the unincorporated hamlet of Sisterdale remained farther south, but the plat in the land office files provides evidence that the upper trail remained in use after traffic on the lower trail ceased. Unless more precise information surfaces, it does not seem unfair to estimate the 1880s as the last days of the upper Pinta Trail.[26]

The trail through the never-to-be Sisterdale stayed in the bottomland of West Sister Creek for roughly five miles before diverting to a western tributary named Jung Creek. It followed that creek's drainage to its headwaters and climbed a challenging ridge before descending into the Grape Creek drainage. The trail trended northwest as it proceeded beyond Grape Creek to the Pedernales.[27]

Individual land surveys do not show the Pinta Trail more than three miles above the Pedernales. Only one expedition mentions the trail above that river: in February 1849, Lieutenant William Henry Chase Whiting traveled from San Antonio to Fredericksburg on a mission to discover a practicable route to El Paso. His report and his diary omit any mention of his path to Fredericksburg, but the Pinta Trail was the only likely option at that date. From his camp on Live Oak Creek, which he said was about five miles from Fredericksburg (the creek runs north-south, three-plus miles to the west of central Fredericksburg), he traveled west for twenty minutes—a mile or so—where he "fell in with an old path known I believe as the Pinta trail, and in former times and to this day used by the Indians." It is not clear from Whiting's diary how far he followed that trail—it may have been a short distance to "a spur of the Piedernales valley," or two miles farther to a "terminating ridge," but no farther. Whiting was accompanied on his expedition by Lieutenant William F. Smith, who noted that the route from Fredericksburg was "partly by the old Pinta trail," without more detail. Although Smith and Whiting did eventually pass by the Presidio San Saba, they did so via an overland route under the guidance of Richard A. Howard, long after leaving the short stretch of trail that might have been the Pinta.[28]

The Whiting and Smith references to the trail are difficult to evaluate. They had almost certainly already been on the trail for several days en route to Fredericksburg, but they only mention the trail farther on, where its existence is uncertain. Whiting makes it clear that he's not entirely confident that he's really on the Pinta. This brief and indefinite reference is the only indication that the trail might have proceeded somewhere to the west of Fredericksburg.

Perhaps more intriguing is an 1847 multiple-survey map done by James P. Hudson of lands north and east of Fredericksburg between the Pedernales and the Llano. That map shows two trails, neither of which is represented by a modern road. To the west is a trail along branches of upper Hickory Creek, running by House Mountain. That is the "Duch [Dutch] Road" built by Emil Kreiwitz so that Adelsverein colonists could reach their land grant. It crosses the Llano River at Elm Creek, about two miles east of Castell. Most surveys along this road are dated from 1845 through 1847. To the east, a second south-north trail passes through a cluster of four 1839 surveys done by James B. Collingsworth and, farther north, through a survey at the foot of Bullhead Mountain done in April 1840 by Jack Hays for his former commander, Henry W. Karnes. The Karnes survey is three miles north of Enchanted Rock, where Jack Hays and his rangers fought Comanches in the autumn of 1841; Hays was reportedly there on a surveying expedition. Simply extending the southern terminus of the trail mapped by Hudson another four-plus miles to the south connects it to the northern terminus of the northward-bound Pinta Trail. Both trails are shown on the 1850 Willke map, which depicts them as originating at Fredericksburg. We know that the Pinta Trail originally passed to the east of the town, but we also know that by 1850 travelers were forsaking the original Pinta Trail ford on the Pedernales in favor of a more direct route to Fredericksburg; this possible upper stretch of the Pinta Trail would likely have been diverted to angle toward the town, too. Without more evidence, however, the connection must remain a hypothesis.[29]

Demise

As mentioned earlier, the lower stretches of the Pinta Trail fell into disuse in the mid-1850s and the trail above Sisterdale was probably abandoned in the 1880s. Below Boerne, it was replaced by a transformation of parts of the old San Saba Road into a new road from San Antonio to Fredericksburg. Below Boerne, the route is mimicked by today's Interstate 10 in places; above Boerne it resembles—but does not match—former Texas State Highway 9, known today as "Old No. 9," which passed through the villages of Welfare and Waring, crossed the Guadalupe near the now-abandoned San Antonio & Aransas Pass Railway bridge, and proceeded up Block Creek toward Fredericksburg. In whole, the route was known in San Antonio as the Fredericksburg Road and to residents of Fredericksburg as the San Antonio Road. (Fredericksburg Road in San Antonio does not follow that earlier route.)

The Fredericksburg Road up Block Creek (Old No. 9) was about seven miles west of Sisterdale. For those who preferred to reach Fredericksburg via the older road from Boerne to Sisterdale, the onward route after the 1880s became today's FM 1376 through Luckenbach.

> For those who want to drive along the route of the Pinta Trail, the news is not good. The trail is approximated by publicly accessible asphalt only for a short distance along San Antonio's Northwest Military Highway outside the gates of Camp Bullis, a stretch of a few hundred yards along Ralph Fair Road in the city of Fair Oaks, and about two miles of FM 1376 above the Guadalupe River.

Conclusion

Old trails simmer with romance and intrigue. They generate legends and lore that sometimes drift away from the facts. The Pinta Trail leading north from San Antonio has long been that sort of pathway, but research into vintage records, assisted by digital mapping tools, allows us to accurately map the old trail as far as the vicinity of Fredericksburg, and reveals tempting clues about its path beyond.

We now know that the Pinta Trail did not follow a modern existing road for any significant distance. It entered the Balcones Escarpment along the pass used by today's Northwest Military Highway, met Salado Creek, and followed that drainage north to Comanche Spring. From there it extended onward to cross Cibolo Creek at Post Oak Creek and to rise into the hills beyond. It turned northwest to cross Spring Creek, Sabinas Creek, and Wasp Creek before fording the Guadalupe River near today's Sisterdale. It followed West Sister Creek to Jung Creek, then proceeded overland to the Grape Creek meadows before mounting another ridge and descending to the Pedernales River, which it forded four-plus miles east of Fredericksburg, near where Zodiac would be established and about two miles mile east of the future Fort Martin Scott. Beyond that point its route is uncertain. One map strongly suggests that the trail continued north to the east of Enchanted Rock and Bullhead Mountain toward the Llano River. The itinerary of Whiting and Smith suggests an alternate possibility— that it might have turned west from Fredericksburg—but the reference is uncertain.

German settlers under the auspices of the Adelsverein colonization company used a shortcut from the Nacogdoches Road to travel from New Braunfels to the Pinta Trail, which they followed to access their new settlement of Fredericksburg, but by 1854 the lower reaches of the trail were abandoned in favor of a more westerly route to Boerne that resembled the Old San Saba Road, and a new road from Boerne to Sisterdale, where the path picked up the Pinta Trail again. Though the upper Pinta Trail remained in use for thirty more years, in the 1880s the Pinta Trail above Sisterdale was abandoned in favor of what has become FM 1376 through Luckenbach. The primary route for traffic from San Antonio to Fredericksburg shifted farther west and became known as the Fredericksburg Road, later to become Texas State Highway 9, which itself has now been overshadowed by Interstate 10 and U.S. Highway 87.

Endnotes

[1] Austin was apparently working from second-hand information: there is no pass there, though the term might apply to either of two small passes on the lower Pinta Trail: the Post Oak Creek defile about five miles farther north, or the canyon through the Balcones Escarpment about nine miles south at today's Northwest Military Highway, west of Salado Creek. Estevan F. Austin, *Mapa original de Texas*, 1829 (Austin: Texas State Library and Archives, map no. 0917). Hermann Willke, *Karte von den Vermessungen im Grant und in der Gegend zwischen demselben und Neu Braunfels*, 1850 (Denton: University of North Texas Libraries, crediting University of Texas at Arlington Library). W. von Rosenberg, *Map of Gillespie County*, 1857 (Austin: Texas General Land Office map 3582, cited hereafter in this format: TGLO map 3582).

[2] The three Cibolo fords mentioned are consistent. Balcones Creek joins Cibolo Creek just above the mouth of Post Oak Creek. Based on all available data, the most frequent crossing point was on the Cibolo, just above Post Oak Creek. John C. Hays, untitled sketch of surveys along the Cibolo, Balcones and Leon Creeks, 1841 (TGLO map 37). John James, untitled sketch of surveys below the porto viejo, 1842? (TGLO map 63). John James, untitled sketch of surveys in the Bexar District along the Guadalupe River and Cibolo Creek, 1846 (TGLO map 3169). Charles deMontel, *Plat of Montel's Surveys on Guadalupe and Sisty's Creek*, 1847 (TGLO map 28682). John James, untitled sketch of surveys along Grape Creek, 1847 (TGLO map 24129), identifies the Pinta Trail just below the Pedernales River as the Fredericksburg Road; at that date, the new road that is referred to in this article as the Fredericksburg Road had not been built.

[3] In 1845, Ferdinand Roemer crossed the Guadalupe where what he called "Cypress Creek" enters the Guadalupe near Cypress Bend. That Cypress Creek is identifiable on old maps as the creek known today as Werner Creek. Ferdinand Roemer and Oswald Mueller, trans., *Texas, with Particular Reference to German Immigration and the Physical Appearance of the Country* (San Antonio: Standard Printing Co., 1935), 220, 225. Osw. Dietz, *Map of Kendall County*, 1862 (TGLO map 3754).

[4] "Ancient Old Spanish Trail leaves prints on modern roads," *West Kerr Current* <http://wkcurrent.com/ancient-old-spanish-trail-leaves-prints-on-modern-roads-p1778-71.htm>.

[5] Nina L. Nixon, "Gillespie County, Texas: The Pinta Trail," Genealogy Trails History Group <http://genealogytrails.com/tex/hillcountry/gillespie/history_pintatrail.html>. Jefferson Morgenthaler, *The German Settlement of the Texas Hill Country*, (Boerne: Mockingbird Books, 2nd ed., 2014), 57. "Pinta Trail," (version prior to 2013) *Handbook of Texas Online* <archival version at

http://web.achive.org/web/20101221000808/http://tshaonline.org/hand book/online/articles/ayp02>.

⁶ Texas Historical Commission (cited hereafter as THC), "The Pinta Trail," THC marker no. 10096, Gillespie County, 1986; THC, "Pinta Trail in Kendall County," THC marker no. 17601, Kendall County, 2013; Ross McSwain, "Early Texas roads evolved from trails," *Transportation News* (Austin: Texas Dept. of Transportation, vol. 28, no. 2, Oct. 2002), 6 <http://ftp.dot.state.tx.us/pub/txdot-info/pio/1002issue.pdf>. Re legends, see J. Frank Dobie, *Coronado's Children* (Austin: University of Texas Press, new ed. 1978) 3-52. Roderick B. Patton, "Miranda's Inspection of Los Almagres: His Journal, Report, and Petition," *Southwestern Historical Quarterly* 47 (Oct. 1970): 223.

⁷ THC, "The Pinta Trail," THC marker no. 10096. THC, "Pinta Trail in Kendall County," THC marker no. 17601. Gillespie County survey no. 32, abst. 386, Juana Isadora Leal, Nov. 12, 1840. Gillespie County survey no. 34, abst. 621, Jose Soto, Nov. 4, 1840. Kendall County survey no. 210, abst. 168, Peter Frazer, Jun. 9, 1846.

⁸ Nicolás de Lafora, "Report of the Journey Made by Don Nicolás de Lafora in Company with Marqués de Rubí to review the Interior Presidios," in George P. Hammond, ed., *The Frontiers of New Spain, Nicolas de Lafora's Description, 1766-1768* (Berkeley: The Quivira Society, 1958), 151-153. Bernardo de Miranda's 1756 expedition in search of the Los Almagres mines appears to have followed Salado Creek to Comanche Spring and from there past the Balcones above Cibolo Creek, but his path veered far east of the Pinta Trail. Patton, "Miranda's Inspection," 236-244.

⁹ Lafora, "Report," 153. Rubí's own account of the trail below the Guadalupe hopelessly mixes the points of the compass, describing a route almost due east. Marqués de Rubí, "Itinerary of Señor Marqués de Rubí," in Jack Jackson, ed. and William C. Foster, intro., *Imaginary Kingdom, Texas as Seen by the Rivera and Rubí Military Expeditions, 1727 and 1767* (Austin: Texas State Historical Association, 1995), 114-118.

¹⁰ De Cordova's well-known 1848 map of Texas shows many of the Pinta Trail landmarks well. J. De Cordova, *J. De Cordova's Map of the State of Texas*, 1848 (TGLO map 7826).

¹¹ James Kimmins Greer, *Texas Ranger, Jack Hays in the Frontier Southwest* (College Station: Texas A&M University Press, 1993), 25, 36.

¹² Kendall County survey no. 1, abst. 96, John D. Colder, Dec. 30, 1839. Hays's report in *Texas National Register*, December 14, 1844, says "on Walker's creek, about fifty miles above Seguin." A letter appearing in *The Northern Standard*, July 24, 1844, (Denton: University of North Texas Libraries, The Portal to Texas History, crediting Dolph Briscoe Center for American History <texashistory.unt.edu/ark:/67531/metapth80523>) from an unnamed writer who claimed to have learned the details of the fight from Hays places it "about four miles east of the Pinto trace, at a point nearly equidistant from Bexar, Gonzaleds [sic] and Austin." Cathe-

rine W. McDowell, ed., *Now You Hear My Horn, The Journal of James Wilson Nichols, 1820-1887* (Austin: University of Texas Press, 1967), 77, says "on the Guadaloupe River at what was then called the Pinta Trail Crossing, it is now the crossing on the road leading from San Antonio to Fredericksburg." J. W. Wilbarger, *Indian Depredations in Texas* (Austin: Hutchings Printing House, 1889), 78, says the fight was at the Pinta Trail crossing of the Guadalupe River without citing a source.

[13] Willke, *Karte.*

[14] Re the colonization contracts of the Adelsverein and Castro generally, see Jefferson Morgenthaler, *Promised Land: Solms, Castro, and Sam Houston's Colonization Contracts* (College Station: Texas A&M University Press, 2009).

[15] Irene Marschall King, *John O. Meusebach, German Colonizer in Texas* (Austin: University of Texas Press, 1967), 154. Alwin Sörgel, *A Sojourn in Texas, 1846-1847* (San Marcos: German-Texan Heritage Society, Southwest Texas State University, 1992), 159.

[16] Roemer, *Texas,* 218-227; Sorgel, *Sojourn,* 156-157; Robert Penniger and Charles L. Wisseman, trans., *Fredericksburg, Texas, the First Fifty Years* (Fredericksburg: Fredericksburg Publishing Co., 1971), 27; Willke, *Karte.* The point where the "old Fredericksburg & New Braunfels road" intercepted the Pinta Trail is shown on Bexar County survey no. 391, abst. 482, Collin C. McCrae, Oct. 4, 1860. The Pinta Trail, which had been abandoned above Cibolo Creek by then, was identified in the survey as "the Comanche Spring San Antonio road." See the discussion of Bartlett's expedition *infra* re Zodiac and Ft. Martin Scott.

[17] Gillespie County survey no. 32, abst. 386, Juana Isadora Leal, Nov. 12, 1840; Gillespie County survey no. 34, abst. 621, Jose Soto, Nov. 4, 1846; Gillespie County survey no. 31, abst. 748, Pedro Jimines, May 20, 1846; Willke, *Karte.*

[18] For example, the following Gillespie County surveys by Jack Hays on Nov. 16, 1840: no. 55, abst. 298, Edward Hodgekin; no. 42, abst. 180, George Debrant; no. 40, abst. 299, Henry Harman. King, *Meusebach,* 73.

[19] Roemer, *Texas,* 220 (first quotation), 227 (second quotation), 220-227.

[20] Francis T. Bryan to Lt. Col. J. E. Johnston, Dec. 1, 1849, in *Reports of the Secretary of War with reconnaissances of routes from San Antonio to El Paso,* 31st Cong., 1st Sess., Ex. Doc. No. 64 (Washington: Union Office, 1850), 15 (quotation), 14-15.

[21] Von Behr is identifiable by comparison to Frederick Law Olmsted, *Journey through Texas, or a Saddle-Trip on the Southwestern Frontier* (New York: Dix, Edwards & Co., 1857), 192-193. The von Behr homestead, identifiable today, is just south of the Guadalupe, which Bartlett crossed next. John Russell Bartlett, *Personal Narrative of Explorations and Incidents in Texas, New Mexico, California, Sonora, and Chihuahua* (New York: D. Appleton & Co., 1854), 59 (first quotation), 60 (second quotation), 47, 53-60.

Zodiac was located about four miles east of Fredericksburg on today's Schmidtzinsky Rd. The tract on which Zodiac was settled was traversed by the Pinta Trail. Gillespie County survey no. 32, abst. 387, Juana Isadora Leal, Nov. 12, 1840. "Fort Martin Scott," *Handbook of Texas Online*, <http://tshaonline.org/handbook/online/articles/qbf33>; "Mormons," *Handbook of Texas Online*, <http://tshaonline.org/handbook/online/articles/ikm01>.

[22] Olmsted, *Journey*, 188 (quotations), 187-202. Presumably the San Saba Road extended to the Presidio San Saba or the San Saba River, but surveys do not show it more than three miles above the Guadalupe. The date that the road from Boerne to Sisterdale was built is uncertain, but it was in use by 1860: Kendall County survey no. 6½, abst. 184, Juan Garcia, Jul. 16, 1860. Note that the 1860 road varies from FM 1376 in the three miles below the Guadalupe River.

[23] Olmsted, *Journey*, 209 (first two quotations), 222 (third quotation), 209-222.

[24] Also note that the Pinta Trail had vanished, but the Fredericksburg Road is shown, on Charles W. Pressler, *Pressler's Map of the State of Texas* (Galveston: Jones, Root and Co., 1858) (TGLO map 76232).

[25] The Guadalupe River crossing demonstrates the shifting nature of trails and roads. Just upstream of the FM 1376 bridge is a discernable old wagon trace across the von Behr farmstead, headed for the river. About 200 yards downstream from the bridge is a cut in the river bank leading to an old, low bridge. Two 1839 surveys show the ford as another 200 yards downstream. Kendall County survey no. 5, abst. 225, William Head, Dec. 4, 1839; Kendall County survey no. 3, abst. 392, Pendleton Rector, Dec. 30, 1839.

[26] C. G. Vogel, untitled sketch enclosed with letter dated Oct. 9, 1879, to the TGLO (TGLO map 28692). Also see W. C. Walsh, TGLO, "Map of Kendall Co., Texas," 1879 (TGLO map 533), though vintage county survey maps, which were traced from one edition to the next, sometimes perpetuate dotted trail lines whether or not the trail continues to exist, and sometimes do not show roads that do exist—the map does not show the Fredericksburg Road, which was built some 25 years earlier. Old county survey maps are more about survey lines than up-to-date road information.

[27] *Sisterdale, TX*, 7.5-Minute Series topographical map (Washington, D.C.: U.S. Geological Survey (cited hereafter as "USGS"), 2013). A 1918 topo map shows the Luckenbach road to the east of FM 1376. *Texas, Fredericksburg Quadrangle*, (USGS, 1918). An 1877 survey shows the "Old Sisterdale and Fredericksburg Road" even farther east. Kendall County survey no. 903, abst. 587, Rusk Transportation Co., Sept. 22, 1877.

[28] William H. C. Whiting, "Whiting Diary," *Publications of the Southern History Association*, vol. IX, no. 6 (Washington, D.C., Nov. 1905), 361, 362 (quote). "Report of Lieut. W. H. C. Whiting, Corps of Engineers, of the exploration of a new route from San Antonio de Bexar to El Paso," June 10,

1849, in *Report of the Secretary of War*, House Ex. Docs., 31 Cong., 1st Sess., vol. 1, no. 1, (Washington: Wm H. Belt, 1850), 281. Wm. F. Smith to J. E. Johnston, May 25, 1849, in *Reports of the Secretary of War with reconnaissances of routes from San Antonio to El Paso*, 31st Cong., 1st Sess., Ex. Doc. No. 64 (Washington: Union Office, 1850), 4. The Whiting Diary also appears in Ralph P. Bieber and Averam B. Bender, *Exploring Southwest Trails* (Glendale: The Arthur H. Clark Co., 1938) at 243, but, as noted in its introduction, that version has been edited, sometimes to its detriment.

[29] James P. Hudson, *Map of Surveys done between the Pedernales & Llano Rivers*, 1847 (TGLO map 11556). The Hickory Creek surveys include Llano County survey no. 24, abst. 669, David Silcriggs, Nov. 1, 1845. The survey that includes House Mountain is Llano County survey no. 93, abst. 501, Matthew Moss, Nov. 7, 1845. Re the "Duch Road," see Llano County survey no. 505, abst. 285, Juana Garcia, Oct. ___, 1847; Llano County survey no. 507, abst. 148, John Y. Criswell, Oct. 7, 1847; and Llano County survey no. 506, abst. 749, William K. Simpson, Oct. 6, 1847. Re Kriewitz, see Emil Kriewitz, "Recollections from Indian Times," in Penniger and Wisseman, *Frederickburg*, 49. Re the Elm Creek ford, see Willke, *Karte* and *Llano, Texas* (USGS, 1992). An example of Collingsworth's surveys is Gillespie County survey no. 2, abst. 719, George W. Ward, Dec. 19, 1839. The Hays survey is Llano County survey no. 11, abst. 444, Henry W. Karnes, Apr. 29, 1840. Re Hays at Enchanted Rock, see Wilbarger, *Indian Depredations*, 74-75 and Greer, *Texas Ranger*, 52. Hays surveyed two other tracts on his trip in the spring of 1840: one for the heirs of Jonah M Lauderdale (Hays was executor of the estate) on April 29, 1840, and another for statesman and former San Antonio mayor William H. Daingerfield on May 28, 1840.